Grand Parenting

Faith That Survives Generations

DR. DAVID JEREMIAH

Grand Parenting

Faith that Survives Generations

Turning Point

with Dr. David Jeremiah

Four generations of Jeremiahs.

Contents

Introduction

If you look for the definition of "grandparent" in the dictionary, you won't find much of an explanation of what it means to be a grandparent—Merriam-Webster's defines a grandparent simply as "a parent of one's father or mother." But I think grandparents are far more than just parents of parents; they are grand parents. The same dictionary gives one definition for "grand" as "intended to impress; very good, wonderful." That's what it means to be a grandparent: we serve a "very good, wonderful" role in our grandchildren's lives.

Most of us don't have great wealth to pass along to our heirs, but some things are more valuable than possessions and wealth. As a grandparent, you can pass along to the next generation something truly priceless: the wisdom that leads to a rich and fulfilling life.

How do we light the correct path for our children and grandchildren to follow? There is a biblical principle that can make a huge difference in the lives of our children and grandchildren. It can be called many things, but I will call it the Law of Deposit and Return. It is found in many verses in the New Testament. Luke 6:38 says it this way: "Give, and it will be given to you: good measure, pressed down, shaken together, and running over will be put into your bosom." And then it concludes: "For with the same measure that you use, it will be measured back to you." The law of investment basically says that the input determines the output. The law also states that we reap what we sow after a period of time (it takes time), and that we reap more than we sow (abundant rewards are possible).

If we do not sow love, for example, into our children and grandchildren, they will not be able to sow what they did not receive into others—and if you want to receive love, you know that you have to invest love. And if we want to see our grandchildren grow up in the fear of the Lord, we must sow those seeds into their lives by teaching and modeling reverence for God. We get what we give.

Some people say we shouldn't try to force our values on our children and grandchildren, but the Bible tells us, "You shall teach [God's commandments] diligently to your children, and shall talk of them when you sit in your house, when you walk by the way, when you lie down, and when you rise up" (Deuteronomy 6:7). In other words, your whole being is to be dedicated to teaching and training and cultivating into the lives of your family the values which you have received from your parents. If we do not influence our families, others will do it for us.

Sharing your faith with your loved ones is a precious and important responsibility that requires the investment of time. In this book we discuss five keys to having a faith that survives generations: faith, family, festivities, fun, and footsteps. I have shared some stories from the Jeremiah family that I hope you will enjoy. At the end of each section are four "legacy" questions that will prompt you to share your story with your grandchildren and future generations, providing them with a family history to treasure.

To have a faith that survives generations, that faith must be convincing, consistent, contagious, and confident. I hope you'll take up that responsibility today with joy and zeal. Remember that your every effort will pay eternal dividends in the lives of your grandchildren.

Dr. David Jeremiah

The righteous man
walks in his integrity;
His children are blessed
after him.

PROVERBS 20:7

A Letter from David & Donna Jeremiah

Donna and I are grandparents to ten wonderful grandchildren.
They call us Nanny and Poppy. This is our message to them.

Dear David Todd, Grace Anne, Bradley, Alexandra,
Makenna, Lauren, Ryland, Hayden, Noelle, and Luke,

We have always heard that being grandparents was a wonderful experience. But we could never have imagined the incredible joy each one of you brings to our hearts. We remember the anticipation we had for your arrival and the excitement we felt the first time we held you in our arms.

David Todd, when you were born, we thought there could never be any love left over for future grandchildren. But guess what? With the addition of each of you, we discovered that while God adds children, He multiplies love.

We pray for each of you and feel so blessed that you are all close by so that we can be part of your lives and participate in your growing-up experiences. God has blessed you all with godly parents and we know that you will bring as much joy to them as they did to us.

We will always be there for you, to spoil you, and then send you back home.

We are truly blessed to be your grandparents . . .

Nanny and Poppy

Therefore know that the LORD your God,
He is God, the faithful God who keeps covenant
and mercy for a thousand generations with those
who love Him and keep His commandments.

DEUTERONOMY 7:9

There is nothing quite so deeply satisfying
as the solidarity of a family united
across the generations and miles
by a common faith and history.

SARA WENGER SHENK

| 1 |

Faith

Grand Parenting
passes the torch of faith
to the next generation.

God Can Use You at Any Age

Sometimes as we get older, we get the impression that we are gradually disappearing from God's radar screen—that we're getting out of the center of what He is doing. But I'm here to tell you that if you read the Bible carefully, you will discover that in the providence of God and in the history of Israel, there was no more powerful nor respected person than the head of the family, which was usually the grandfather or perhaps even the great-grandfather. The Bible placed the grandfather in a place of great honor, and his words were considered sacred by his children and grandchildren.

One such grandfather in the Old Testament was Jacob. Jacob had many children and many grandchildren, but the last scene of Jacob's life was a scene of blessing and worship shared by two of his grandsons, Ephraim and Manasseh (Genesis 48:1–20). It made a lasting impression on his son Joseph, and on his grandsons as well.

Hebrews 11:21 tells us that "By faith Jacob, when he was dying, blessed each of the sons of Joseph, and worshiped, leaning on the top of his staff." Even to his dying day, Jacob held on to faith and passed that steadfast belief in God along to his grandchildren. It is just as true for today that we can pass along a heritage of faith and belief to those who follow after us.

So don't lose heart. Your role in your family's life is priceless. Scripture tells us to "make the most of every opportunity" (Colossians 4:5 NIV). Take advantage of every chance you get to tell your grandchildren you love them, to teach them about the faith that means so much to you, to blaze a trail for them to follow in life. Most importantly, pray prayers of blessing over your family, just as Jacob did. Your children and grandchildren will reap greater rewards than any of you will see in this lifetime.

So we, Your people and sheep of Your pasture,
Will give You thanks forever; We will show forth
Your praise to all generations.

PSALM 79:13

13

A Family Legacy

When he closed his eyes [for the last time], that's when I realized the gift that he gave to me, the gift that he was going to be with His Lord and Savior, Jesus Christ. He had, back in 1988 on a flight from Washington, D.C. to Point Mugu, told me about his love of God, his love of Christ as his Savior. I didn't know then what it all meant. But I certainly do now.

I can't think of a better gift for a father to give a son. And I hope to honor my father by giving my son Cameron and my daughter Ashley that same gift he gave to me.

MICHAEL REAGAN,
IN MEMORIAL OF HIS FATHER, RONALD W. REAGAN,
THE FORTIETH PRESIDENT OF THE UNITED STATES
TAKEN FROM WWW.RONALDREAGANMEMORIAL.COM

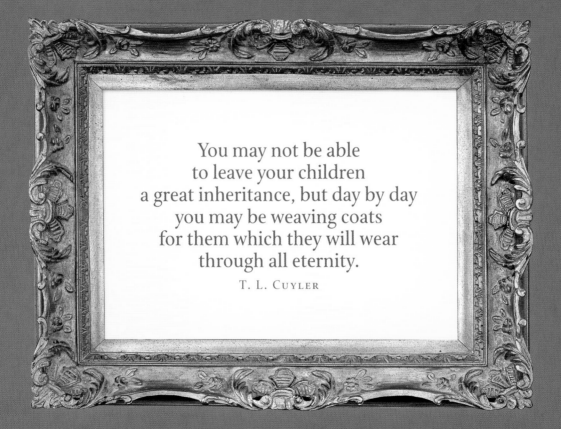

You may not be able
to leave your children
a great inheritance, but day by day
you may be weaving coats
for them which they will wear
through all eternity.

T. L. CUYLER

Generational Messages

I can say that today I am a blessed man. My parents weren't perfect by any means, but what they contributed to my life by virtue of their love for Jesus Christ and their commitment to see us grow up in a faith that was based upon the Word of God—I could never ever repay them for that. And I rise up and call them blessed.

David Paul Jeremiah

In looking back at my relationship with my grandparents, there is a common thread that reaches through both sides of the family and both sets of grandparents. That thread is time spent together. Living in California meant that we did not live near our grandparents and did not have the opportunity to spend time with them every week. However, both sets would spend time with us in California to get away from the cold Midwest and Northeast winters. As I think back, the memories that are the strongest are memories of our time together; however simple the activities, it was about just being together.

Every time that my father's parents came to California, they would take each one of us out to eat individually. I can still remember these times like they were yesterday. We would go to Denny's and I could have whatever I wanted for breakfast. I remember one time they let me order fried chicken for breakfast. I can still see the look on Grandpa's face when they set the plate down in front of me.

When my mother's parents would come to California, they would stay in our home with us. I remember many hours sitting at the kitchen table and playing dominoes with them and eating whatever freshly baked goodies Grandma had made that day. The games were fun, but they did not compare to the cookies!

What a great reminder to me as a parent; it is about spending time together!

DAVID MICHAEL JEREMIAH

My nanny and poppy are very special to me. One of the ways my poppy is special is because he is a pastor. He teaches God's Word to people. My poppy also writes many good books, and he has one best-selling book, *What in the World Is Going On?* He and Nanny take the time to take me to interesting places. A cool thing about my poppy is that he is funny and tells a lot of jokes, and Nanny is always willing to play a game with me. My nanny and poppy are very interesting in many ways, and I love them.

DAVID TODD JEREMIAH

Three generations of David Jeremiah

Silver Lining
The Wisdom That Comes With Age

I have noticed a real difference in my generation and my father's generation. When I was growing up, there was a seriousness about life and the faith that is missing today. I would never have asked if I could stay home from church, for example. It would have seemed to me— and to my parents—like committing a cardinal sin.

Today we say we're relaxed, not legalistic. But I wonder if we've lost something over the years. And if we have, then what will happen in my children's and grandchildren's generations—will they keep the faith? That's something we as parents and grandparents need to consider as we test our hearts to see if our faith is as genuine as the faith of those who came before us.

I have found one way to bless my grandchildren is to give them a legacy of prayer. As Samuel said to the Israelites, "Far be it from me that I should sin against the LORD in ceasing to pray for you" (1 Samuel 12:23).

I pray for my grandchildren regularly. I pray that God will protect them and keep them, that He would help them grow up to know Jesus Christ. I remember the day my oldest grandchild, David Todd, called me on the phone and told me he had accepted Jesus into his heart. It was an answer to my prayers.

Beyond your fervent prayers for your grandchildren, perhaps the greatest gift that you can give is to model before them a life committed to Christ, showing them what a Christian is by your actions and words. Then, as you pass on the legacy of faith, your blessing will be the greatest final gift you can give to your heirs.

We give thanks to the God and Father
of our Lord Jesus Christ, praying always for you.
COLOSSIANS 1:3

Children are a bridge to heaven.

PERSIAN PROVERB

Laugh Lines

A grandson was spending time with his grandfather one day and asked, "Grandpa, do you know how you and God are alike?"

Grandpa brightened a little. *That's not something you hear every day,* he thought. "No," he answered, "how are we alike?"

"You're both old," he replied.

•

Grandparents defined from an eight-year-old child's perspective:

WHAT IS A GRANDPARENT?

- Grandparents are a lady and a man who have no little children of their own. They like other peoples.
- A grandfather is a man grandmother.
- Grandparents don't have to do anything except be there when we come to see them. They are so old they shouldn't play hard and run. It is good if they drive us to the store and have lots of quarters for us.
- They don't say, "Hurry up."
- Grandparents don't have to be smart. But they have to answer questions like "Why isn't God married?"
- When they read to us, they don't skip. They don't mind if we ask for the same story again and again.
- They know we should have snack time before bedtime, and they say prayers with us every time, and kiss us even when we've acted bad.
- When they take us for walks, they slow down by things like pretty leaves and caterpillars.

Share God's Word

Does your grandchild have a great study Bible? If not, a gift Bible would be a wonderful way for you to share your faith with them. Select something at your favorite Christian store, and write a note inside telling them how much God's Word has meant to you over the years. Personalize it with their name and the date and present it as a special gift.

Even better, if you have a family Bible, sit down with your grandchildren and go through it with them. Tell them about their great-grandparents and great-great-grandparents. Point out special days in your family's history and tell them about your religious roots. But most importantly, point out which verses of Scripture meant the most to you and your family at certain times in your life, and why. That way, they'll catch a glimpse at how an active faith has sustained and shaped you throughout your life.

A Loving Legacy

Use these pages to record some details of your journey of faith to help you share that journey with your grandchildren.

This is how I came to know about Christ and placed my trust in Him.

_____

_____

_____

_____

_____

_____

_____

The most influential person in my journey of faith was:

_____

_____

_____

_____

My favorite passage of Scripture is:

_____

_____

_____

_____

The one thing that I want my children and grandchildren to understand about being a Christian is:

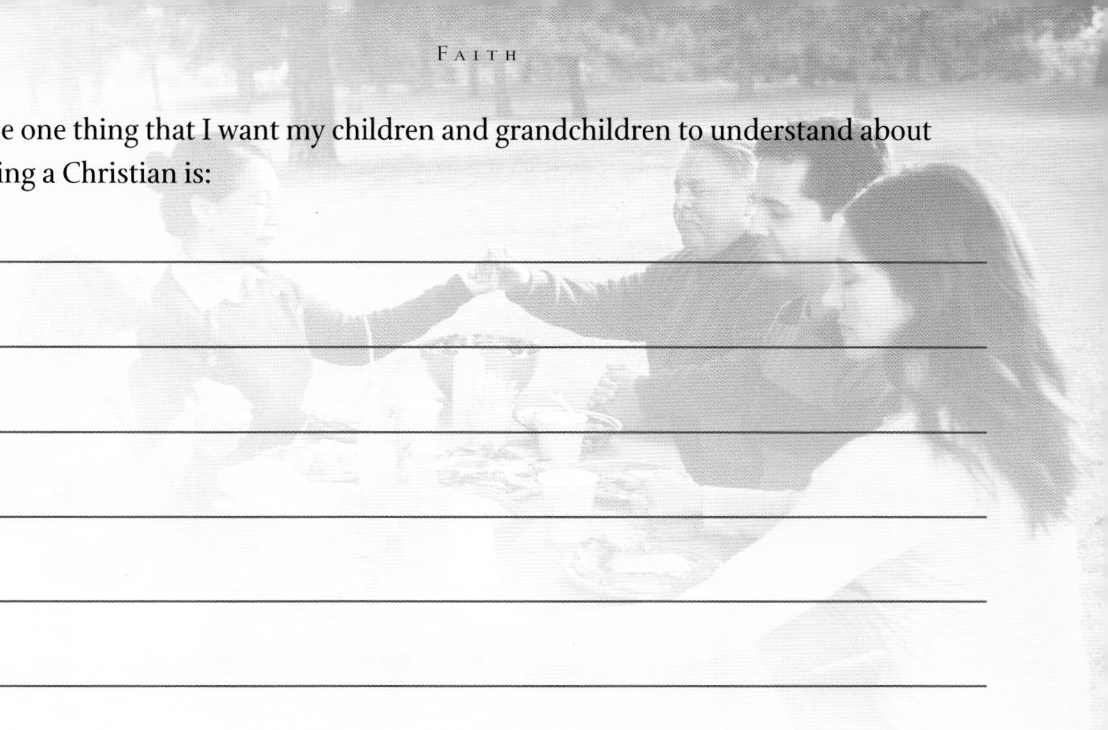

_____

_____

_____

_____

_____

_____

_____

_____

_____

Lord, *You have been
our dwelling place
in all generations.*

Psalm 90:1

A Prayer from the Heart

Dear Heavenly Father, thank You for Your faithfulness to me—You have given me a great story to tell. I pray that You would help me share that story with my grandchildren, not only in words, but in how I live my life. Help me seize opportunities to tell them about You, and help me share Your love with them. I ask that You would open their hearts to see You and know You.

In Jesus' name, Amen.

Great is the Lord,
and greatly to be praised;
And His greatness
is unsearchable.
One generation
shall praise Your works
to another, And shall
declare Your mighty acts.

PSALM 145:3–4

Grandchildren are the dots
that connect the lines
from generation to generation.

LOIS WYSE

| 2 |

Family

Grand Parenting is the glue
that holds families together.

Fulfilling Your Family's Purpose

One of Norman Rockwell's famous paintings shows a beaming father looking down on a proud son who has just smashed his way through a rock of a would-be tackler to score a touchdown in a big game—leaving a few of his teeth behind in the process.

You can't help but smile when you see this warmhearted image of days gone by. Something deep within us revels in family scenes where parents delight in their children, and where those children take pride in Mom and Dad. The family is God's idea. If God created family, then doesn't it make sense that He might have something to say about how we can make it work? The first step is, "Unless the Lord builds the house, they labor in vain who build it" (Psalm 127:1).

According to Scripture, parenting is a two-way street. Proverbs looks at healthy families from divergent perspectives. In Proverbs 17:6 we read, "Parents are the pride of their children" (NIV), while Proverbs 23:24 declares, "The father of a righteous man has great joy; he who has a wise son delights in him" (NIV).

You know you have a healthy family when the children and grandchildren take pride in their parents and grandparents. Modeling is an important part of the process. As your children see you take pride, and show respect and courtesy to your parents, respect for grandparents is built into the family relationships. Good role models provide great results.

God has a wonderful plan for your family. When you cooperate with His leading, you'll grow closer and closer to Him and to each other.

Behold, how good and how pleasant it is
For brethren to dwell together in unity!

PSALM 133:1

The Way of Wisdom

Have you ever looked ahead to the future generations of your family and purposed to leave a godly heritage to bear fruit long after you are gone from this earth? In 2 Timothy 1:5, Paul reminds Timothy of the faith that came to him through his grandmother Lois and his mother Eunice. It may be further than our grandchildren by which our legacy is truly determined. We in this generation should purpose to build on what God can do through us for the sake of future generations.

Some people have wondered if I am descended from a long line of preachers—and the answer is no. My father was the first in his family to serve Christ, but he became so excited about the Lord that he gave his life to ministry. He purposed to turn around a family heritage that he had received which was not spiritual and thereby change the future. I grew up with faith in Christ and now our children have faith in Christ. And before he died, my father's father also placed his faith in Christ.

With family, one person in one generation can make a difference for generations to follow.

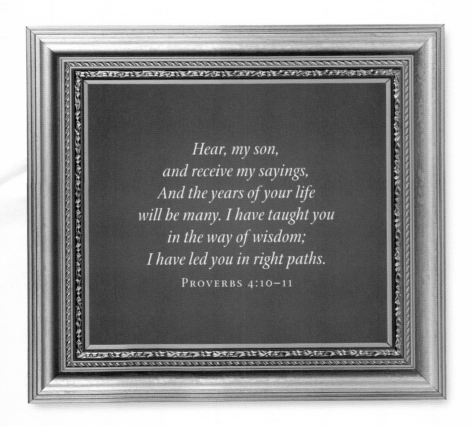

Hear, my son,
and receive my sayings,
And the years of your life
will be many. I have taught you
in the way of wisdom;
I have led you in right paths.

PROVERBS 4:10–11

Grandparents are
a delightful blend
of laughter,
caring deeds,
wonderful stories,
and love.

AUTHOR UNKNOWN

The "Be" Attitudes for Grandchildren

Some words of wisdom to share with your grandchildren.

AUTHOR UNKNOWN

- Be understanding to your enemies. Be loyal to your friends.
- Be strong enough to face the world each day. Be weak enough to know you cannot do everything alone.
- Be generous to those who need your help. Be frugal with what you need yourself.
- Be wise enough to know that you do not know everything. Be foolish enough to believe in miracles.
- Be willing to share your joys. Be willing to share in the sorrows of others.
- Be a leader when you see a path others have missed. Be a follower when you are shrouded by the mists of uncertainty.
- Be first to congratulate an opponent who succeeds. Be last to criticize a colleague who fails.
- Be sure where your next step will fall, so that you will not stumble. Be sure of your final destination in case you are going the wrong way.
- Be loving to those who love you. Be loving to those who do not love you; they may change.
- Be yourself.

Silver Lining:
The Wisdom That Comes With Age

One of the most often-quoted verses in the Bible is taken from Joshua's final words to the Israelites: "And if it seems evil to you to serve the LORD, choose for yourselves this day whom you will serve, whether the gods which your fathers served that were on the other side of the River, or the gods of the Amorites, in whose land you dwell. But as for me and my house, we will serve the LORD" (Joshua 24:15).

Even in his old age Joshua was a father who took responsibility for the spiritual legacy of his own family. That is what our nation and our churches need as much as anything I can think of—men who will say, "As for me and my house, we will serve the Lord." Men who will step up and declare themselves the lovers and defenders of their marriages and families.

Don't lose the sensitivity in your home to the fact that you are a role model. What you say, what you watch on television, how you treat others—it is all being watched by your children and grandchildren even if you are unaware of their watchful eyes.

May God give you the courage to be in an ever-changing world without being of it.

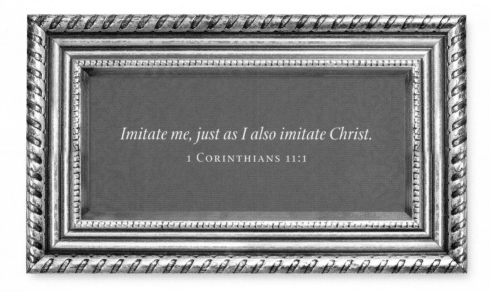

Imitate me, just as I also imitate Christ.

1 CORINTHIANS 11:1

Laugh Lines

A grandmother is a babysitter who
watches the kids instead of the television.

AUTHOR UNKNOWN

•

Grandchildren don't stay young forever, which is good
because Pop-Pops have only so many horsey rides in them.

GENE PERRET

•

A little boy's grandmother always defined her age as "twenty-nine and hold-ing." So when his mother celebrated her thirtieth birthday, he realized something didn't add up. "Mom, you're thirty, and Grandma's twenty-nine," he said, sound-ing puzzled. Then he concluded, "I guess you must have been adopted."

•

All of Turning Point was celebrating Dr. Jeremiah's birthday in the lunchroom. His grandson, David Todd, whispered in his ear, "How old are you today, Poppy?" Those at the adjoining tables leaned closer as Dr. Jeremiah whispered, "65." Forgetting to whisper, David Todd shouted, "Wow, if you were a dog, you'd be dead!"

Family Tree Activity

One of the most popular hobbies in America is the study of one's genealogy. There are many books at your local library and a plethora of online tools to assist you in tracing your lineage and finding out more about your ancestors.

A full blown study may or may not hold interest for you, but for a simple half-hour or hour-long activity to do with your grandchildren, start with a blank poster board and some markers. Now sketch out a family tree starting with them, and go up as many levels as you can from memory. As you write down names, dates, and places from memory, tell a little about each person. This would be a great opportunity to tell about family members that were strong in faith—but a little humor would be good to hear as well!

But won't this bore them? My grandchildren are hooked on video games!

Maybe your grandchild will follow a script that says this is something they aren't interested in and show some boredom. Just have a little confidence and a good sense of humor and you will be amazed at how interested they really are in where they came from. Whether they express immediate appreciation or not, your words will sink into their hearts. And who knows, maybe you'll be the one who has to say the activity is finished!

A Loving Legacy

Use these pages to record special memories of your family.

Our ancestors came from these parts of the world.

_____

_____

_____

_____

_____

_____

_____

_____

This is a description of my parents. This is where they were born. They were (fun, serious, punctual, kind). My father worked as a . . . My mother was . . . The most important thing I learned from my parents was:

_____

_____

_____

_____

_____

_____

_____

This is how I met my sweetheart, fell in love, and became engaged.

_____

_____

_____

_____

_____

_____

_____

_____

_____

_____

Our Grandchildren

_____

_____

_____

_____

_____

Our Great-Grandchildren

_____

_____

_____

_____

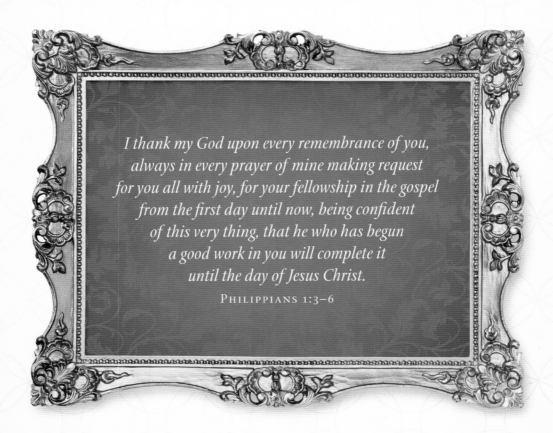

*I thank my God upon every remembrance of you,
always in every prayer of mine making request
for you all with joy, for your fellowship in the gospel
from the first day until now, being confident
of this very thing, that he who has begun
a good work in you will complete it
until the day of Jesus Christ.*

PHILIPPIANS 1:3–6

A Prayer from the Heart

Dear Heavenly Father, thank You for the blessing of my family. I know that I am not perfect and that we are not perfect, but the children and grandchildren You've given me are the greatest blessing in my life, and I love them. Knit us together with Your love, Father, and continue Your work in our lives to make us more loving and more patient toward each other. Show me how I can best help my children, and what You have for me to offer my grandchildren. Be our guide and protector as a family, Lord God, and teach us to love You more each day.

In Jesus' name, Amen.

A merry heart does good, like medicine,
But a broken spirit dries the bones.

PROVERBS 17:22

There is nothing higher and stronger
and more wholesome and useful for life
in later years than some good memory,
especially a memory connected
with childhood, with home.

FYODOR DOSTOYEVSKY

| 3 |

Festivities

Grand Parenting creates
memorable moments.

Family Traditions

Every family has its own traditions for celebrating the holidays, whether it means opening your gifts on Christian Eve, or eating ham on Easter Sunday. Those traditions for celebrating special days become part of the memories your children and grandchildren will treasure—playing games together after a large family dinner, or perhaps taking a nice walk together, or playing a friendly family basketball game. These times are precious, and planning for special festivities makes these moments even more memorable.

A longstanding holiday tradition in the Jeremiah household is the annual jigsaw puzzle. We get a new one each year, one with a gazillion pieces, and work on it throughout the Christmas holiday season. All the pieces are spread out on a table that is reserved solely for the holiday puzzle. Various Jeremiahs will stop and try a few pieces until the picture is finally completed. (I won't reveal what percent of these puzzles have been fully completed over the years.)

We've found puzzles to be a great diversion when friends and family are gathered—something we can build together. And they offer a good opportunity to exercise our puzzle-solving skills as a family.

We always get the sides finished first—with all the edge pieces in place, we have a nice frame in which to build the picture. Corners and straight edges are simple—it's what's in the middle that gives us trouble.

In the puzzles of life, we are often able to work out the borders of things—the places where life is straight, where the corners meet neatly. But to solve the big picture, we need wisdom, persistence, and perhaps the help of loved ones.

Your family probably has its own traditions, completely different from ours. They might be serious or silly, funny or poignant. That's okay. All that matters is that you spend time together creating memories, ones that will stay in your grandchildren's hearts and minds forever, giving them a solid foundation on which to build their lives.

Oh, magnify the LORD with me,
And let us exalt His name together.

PSALM 34:3

Silver Lining:
The Wisdom That Comes With Age

In 1994, my husband and partner, the father of my children, was diagnosed with lymphoma. There is never a good time for bad news; but with God's help and the love of our family and friends, we made it through that bend in the road. Though it is now fifteen years later, and David is in great health, during those dark days as a wife and mother, I found that it really helped to keep life as normal as possible. Celebrating holidays and birthdays, attending sports events, and mingling with our church family kept me hopeful. Those special times became even more memorable because of the reality that those moments might not always be possible. I encourage each family to treasure your special moments together—they are gifts from the Lord.

DONNA JEREMIAH

Blueberry Cake

This special recipe from Donna Jeremiah is enjoyed by her children and grandchildren at family events.

½ CUP BUTTER

½ CUP SUGAR

¼ TEASPOON SALT

1 TEASPOON VANILLA EXTRACT

2 EGG YOLKS

1½ CUPS FLOUR

1 TEASPOON BAKING POWDER

⅓ CUP MILK

2 EGG WHITES

¼ CUP SUGAR

1½ CUPS FRESH BLUEBERRIES

1 TABLESPOON FLOUR

¼ CUP SUGAR

1 TABLESPOON SUGAR

Preheat oven to 350 degrees and grease and flour an eight-inch pan.

Cream butter and ½ cup sugar until fluffy. Add salt and vanilla. Separate eggs and reserve the whites. Add egg yolks to the sugar mixture; beat until creamy.

Combine 1½ cups flour and baking powder; add alternately with milk to egg yolk mixture. Coat berries with 1 tablespoon flour and add to batter.

In a separate bowl, beat whites until soft peaks form. Add ¼ cup sugar a tablespoon at a time, and beat until stiff peaks form. Fold egg whites into batter. Pour into prepared pan. Sprinkle top with remaining 1 tablespoon sugar.

Bake for 50 minutes or until done.

Laugh Lines

GRANDMA GOES TO THE POST OFFICE

A woman went to the post office to buy stamps for her Christmas cards. "What denomination?" asked the clerk.

"Oh, good heavens! Have we come to this?" said the woman. "Well, give me thirty Baptist, ten Catholic, twenty Lutheran, and forty Presbyterian."

•

A little boy asked his grandmother what year she was born. She told him she was born in 1935.

"Wow!" the boy exclaimed. "If you were a baseball card, you'd be worth lots of money."

•

GRANDMA'S HOME

When I stopped the bus to pick up Chris for preschool, I noticed an older woman hugging him as he left the house. "Is that your grandmother?" I asked.

"Yes," Chris said. "She's come to visit us for Christmas."

"How nice," I said. "Where does she live?"

"At the airport," Chris replied. "Whenever we want her, we just go out there and get her."

Our children need to hear
from us how special they are,
and they need to hear it in terms
they both understand and believe.

D A V I D J E R E M I A H

Make a Memory

The next time your family gathers around one of your traditions—whether it's a game night, a special movie you watch together, or that Thanksgiving turkey—freeze the moment in time by taking a group photo. Then have a copy made for each of your grandchildren and send it to them in a small frame (even an inexpensive one will do nicely, especially if you decorate it yourself). Include a message you want them to remember from your heart.

Now if you're really excited about this idea, begin building a memory book based on family get-togethers for each of your grandchildren. Imagine what a present that would make for an eighteenth birthday or a high school graduation!

Whether it's a simple framed picture or an elaborate scrapbook, you'll reinforce beloved family traditions and give your grandchildren a precious keepsake.

A Loving Legacy

Use these pages to record memorable family activities.

As a child growing up, this is how we celebrated birthdays:

_____

_____

_____

_____

_____

_____

_____

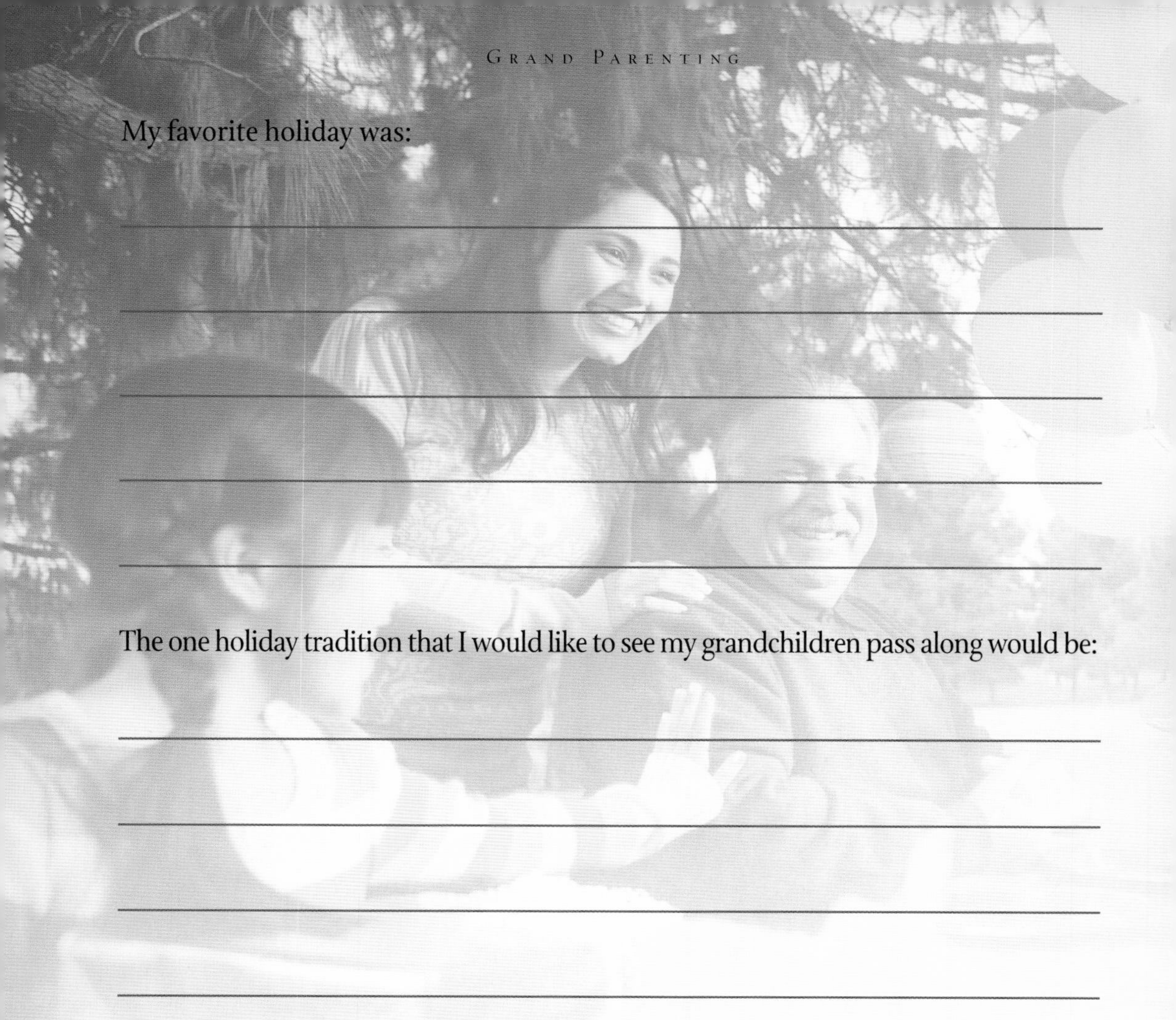

My favorite holiday was:

_____

_____

_____

_____

The one holiday tradition that I would like to see my grandchildren pass along would be:

_____

_____

_____

_____

The food that I associate with happy family memories is:

_____

_____

_____

_____

_____

*Let us come
before His presence
with thanksgiving;
Let us shout joyfully
to Him with psalms.*

PSALM 95:2

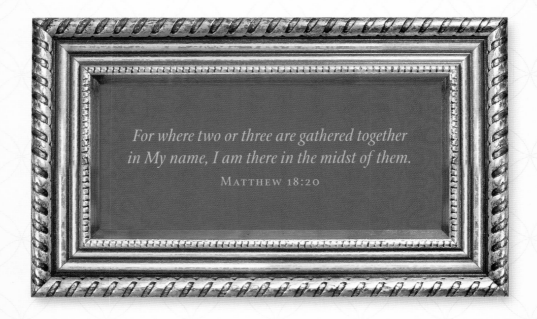

For where two or three are gathered together in My name, I am there in the midst of them.

MATTHEW 18:20

A Prayer from the Heart

Dear Heavenly Father, I know that You are pleased when Your people gather together—how much more pleased You must be to see families spending time together. Lord, I pray for Your presence at our next family gathering. Season our interactions with Your grace and help us to take delight in each other, the way You take delight in each of us. Give me ideas and wisdom about how to create a fun, memorable time for my grandchildren. And may Your traveling mercies be with us as we journey to be together.

In Jesus' name, Amen.

Rejoice in the Lord always.
Again I will say, rejoice!

PHILIPPIANS 4:4

A happy home
is more than a roof
over your head;
it's a foundation
under your feet.

AUTHOR UNKNOWN

| 4 |

Fun

Grand Parenting
fills our lives with joy.

Sharing Life

Enjoying your grandchildren doesn't require a special occasion, or even a lot of money—time spent together is the key.

I didn't know my grandfathers very well—my grandfather on my mother's side died when I was quite young—but I did get to know my grandfather on my father's side a little bit. He was quite a character.

One of my fondest memories of him was his willingness to include me in his life. When I was a little boy, we used to visit my grandparents in Johnson City, New York. My grandfather was the head custodian of the Johnson City schools, and he had keys to all the buildings. When I would come for a visit, which was usually during the Christmas holidays, he would take me to work with him. And since this was the Christmas season and school wasn't in session, he would take me to the gym, get some basketballs out of the closet, and throw them on the floor, saying, "Go to it, son. It's all yours." I had that whole gym to myself to play basketball, which is probably one of the reasons why I grew up loving that game and playing it a great deal.

He would watch, make a few comments, and then go to his rounds. Then he would come back and pick me up, and we would usually stop and get something to eat on the way home. We didn't talk too much, and our visits were somewhat infrequent, so I suppose I didn't know my grandfather very well. But I did know that he loved me and that he took me under his wing and shared his life with me as best he could.

That's one of the things that grandparents can do: we can share our lives. We can include our grandchildren in what we do. We can share with them who we are. And we have a lot to give, believe me—a lot that is needed in this generation. We can share much-needed values with our grandchildren by living transparently in front of them, values that may be lacking in this culture and time. And the time we spend with them can also give them a vital sense of security and stability.

There's another value to spending time with our grandchildren, of course: it's fun. When that first grandchild was born, your heart probably nearly exploded with joy. As you do even simple, everyday things with them, that joy multiplies. So don't underestimate the value of just being together. It's one of the happiest—and most valuable—things in a grandparent's life.

Therefore comfort each other
and edify one another,
just as you also are doing.
1 THESSALONIANS 5:11

Fun Things to Do
With Your Grandchildren

Your grandchildren love to be with you, and there is no shortage of things you can do together. Here are a few ideas to get you started.

- Take a nature walk together
- Play ball
- Show them how to skip or jump rope
- Teach them how to play a game
- Get out coloring books and crayons and color with them
- Take a multigenerational vacation
- Teach them to crochet or knit
- Make a sandbox for your yard out of a giant tractor tire
- Teach them to cook a favorite recipe
- Take them to a family reunion
- Volunteer to help at their school
- Tell them stories about your life
- Make birthdays a special event
- Share your treasures and memorabilia with them
- Introduce them to something you like such as music, a type of food, or a special sport

A good laugh is
as good as a prayer
sometimes.

LUCY MAUD MONTGOMERY

Silver Lining
The Wisdom That Comes With Age

It's vital for grandparents to be as accessible as possible. Do all you can to spend time with your grandchildren. Open your home and your schedule. Make your house kid-friendly. Talk to them, tell them stories, and read them Scripture.

Of course, in our mobile society, many people do not live near their grandchildren. But a week here or there, a vacation, a stream of letters, e-mails, webcam visits, and regular phone calls can help fill in the gap. Some grandparents even record bedtime stories, and their grandchildren go to bed every evening listening to their grandparents' voices.

Sometimes grandparents can help provide materially for their grandchildren. Just a little bit here and there. Clothing. Books. Toys. Tools for a hobby. A little seed money for college. Many young families are financially stressed, and a few extras along the way from a loving grandparent can make a big difference.

You have a lot to offer your grandchildren. Take some time to show them your love today.

Food for Thought

"The bond between a child and a grandparent is the purest, least psychologically complicated form of human love," says Dr. Arthur Kornhaber, author of several books on grandparenting. He claims that grandparents can offer an emotional safety net when parents falter. They pass on traditions in the form of stories, songs, games, skills, and crafts. And they often have another magical ingredient that parents sometimes lack—time.

There you have it: all those afternoons of horsey rides and playing make-believe barber shop are priceless in the lives of your grandchildren. What you do matters!

Laugh Lines

One weekend, a little boy came to stay with his grandmother. Early in the morning, he came into her room with a cup of coffee he had made himself. She thanked him and took a sip—and it was terrible. But she gulped it down anyway. And when she had drunk all but the last few inches of coffee, she noticed two plastic army figures in the bottom of the cup.

"Now why would there be two little army guys in my cup?" she asked him.

"Oh, you know," said the little boy. "It's like they say on television. The best part of waking up is soldiers in your cup."

•

One afternoon, a grandmother and her granddaughter spent the day together at a park. Grandma decided to test her granddaughter to see if she had learned her colors yet. She pointed out different objects in the park and asked what color they were. The little girl got them right every time, but the grandma kept going, even after they'd been through all the colors once or twice.

Finally, she pointed out a yellow road sign, and the little girl said, "Grandma, I think you should try to figure out some of these for yourself!"

The Gift of Your Time

Maybe you're blessed with many grandchildren, or maybe you have just a few. In either case, a precious gift you can give each

one of them is a little of your time. This month, try to take each of your grandchildren out on a one-on-one "date." (And when you pick them up, it might be good to explain to their siblings that they'll be getting their own special Grandma or Grandpa time soon.) Go out for ice cream or go to the park. No need to make fancy plans; all you need to do is give them a little focused attention. If your grandchildren live far away, make a call to speak to one grandchild. The time spent will be priceless. Rest assured, they will remember this day or conversation forever. Just one afternoon may give them a dose of love and security that will serve them their entire lives.

A Loving Legacy

Use these pages to record fun memories from your life.

Some of my favorite games, toys, or ways to entertain myself as a child and teenager were:

_____

_____

_____

The "in" things of my youth (clothing styles, colors, hairstyles, slang, etc.) were:

_____

_____

_____

_____

A special memory of childhood that was particularly fun and that I enjoyed doing was:

_____

_____

_____

_____

A special time that I remember with my grandparents was:

_____

_____

_____

_____

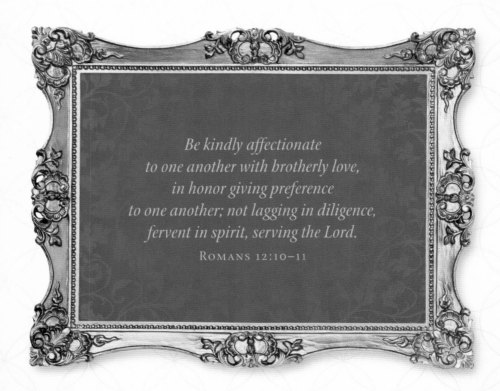

*Be kindly affectionate
to one another with brotherly love,
in honor giving preference
to one another; not lagging in diligence,
fervent in spirit, serving the Lord.*

ROMANS 12:10–11

A Prayer from the Heart

Dear Heavenly Father, thank You for each member of my family, and for the joy they bring me. You have blessed me beyond my belief, God. Please help me each day see my family members as the blessing that they are. Be with us as I spend time with them, Lord God, and help us to rejoice in You together.

In Jesus' name, Amen.

Children's children are a crown to the aged.

PROVERBS 17:6 NIV

We all belong to another world,
to another time,
to another place of long ago.
I believe it is important
to share your history with those
you love so that they
will be able to tell their children
about the foundation of their lives.

CHRISTOPHER DE VINCK

| 5 |

Footsteps

Grand Parenting leaves a legacy.

For Generations to Come

The legacy that we leave behind for generations to come begins with our walk with God. Do you talk about things of the Lord with your children and grandchildren? Do they know about your daily Bible study and prayer life? All of this is setting an example for them to follow. Our faith is the cornerstone, but there are other qualities we might possess that our heirs may wish to emulate, such as our temperament or our work ethic.

Children and grandchildren look at what our values are; they look at the things we do. Some families try to replace time spent together with material possessions. The question is not whether your family will be influenced by the culture and its values, but how much influence it will have. Someone has said that you can never be judged as a parent until you evaluate the lives of your grandchildren. The values that we place in our children are the values by which they will raise their families. And so the life of our investment is not just one generation, but it is generation after generation—like footsteps in the sand. The values that our children emulate and develop become strong commitments and convictions in their lives as they raise our grandchildren and generations to follow.

My mother, Ruby Jeremiah, was an amazing woman. She kept a scrapbook for each of her four children and her husband long before "scrapbooking" was popular. She often hosted people in her home, even after a day of working in the printing room at the college where my father was president. I am not saying my mother was a perfect woman, but she did have a spirit that said nothing is beneath the dignity of a person who loves her family and loves the work. Whatever needed to be done, she found a way to do it.

My mother was also a woman of prayer. One of the things I remember most vividly is seeing her come out of her room with tears on her cheeks after communing with God in prayer. Seeing the faith of both my mother and father lived out in the challenges of daily life had a strong impact on me. I want to tell you that seeing an example like that marks you for life.

An unknown poet wrote these words:

> I saw you stand bravely through the years
> And saw no sign of senseless fears
> I saw you stand quietly through the stress
> And saw no glimpse of bitterness
> I saw you stand prayerfully in grief
> And saw no sign of unbelief
> Though you spoke well of Jesus Christ
> I caught your faith by watching your life

When we talk about being a servant-hearted person, what that means is simply that the spirit of serving comes naturally from an overflowing heart of love to the people who are on our love list. My mom was like that, and I rise up today and call her blessed. I want to follow in her footsteps and model those footsteps for my children and grandchildren in the future.

My parents had a strong influence on my life. That's not only true in my life, it's true in the lives of my children. And if you want to be a strong influence in your family, it isn't too late to make a difference.

You shall teach them
diligently to your children,
and shall talk of them
when you sit in your house,
when you walk by the way,
when you lie down,
and when you rise up.

DEUTERONOMY 6:7

An Irish Grandparent Blessing

For love lavished beyond measure,
For happy hours always to treasure,
For bounteous meals at holiday season,
For wealth of memories beyond all reason,
For quality of life that examples impart.
I love my Irish grandparents with all my heart.

Silver Lining
The Wisdom That Comes With Age

Whatever we do in the lives of our children and grandchildren in their early days will have the greatest influence on who they become when their adulthood arrives and their values and maturity set in. So, just like a seed that is sown in the ground, it takes a while for that seed to germinate and to ultimately bear fruit; what we are doing in the lives of our family has a long fuse on it. We work at it and work at it. Sometimes it's discouraging. Sometimes we wonder if the investment is really having an effect, if maybe we should have stayed at work where there was peace and quiet instead of coming home early so often to spend time with the family. The time invested will yield positive results. Whatever you want your children and grandchildren to be, you need to cultivate that in the lives of your family.

Every material goal,
even if it is met,
will pass away.
But the heritage
of children is timeless.
Our children are our
messages to the future.

BILLY GRAHAM

A child's hand in yours—what
tenderness and power it arouses.
You are instantly the very touchstone
of wisdom and strength.

MARJORIE HOLMES

Ten Ways to Love
Your Grandchildren

- Establish boundaries for their lives
- Enjoy them
- Expose your humanness to them
- Explain the reasons behind your decisions
- Exchange ideas with them
- Encourage them
- Embolden them to believe they can go further than they dream
- Express physically what you feel in your heart
- Examine your own life regularly
- Exercise great patience with them

Food for Thought

Grandparents are the oral historians of the family. One of my favorite stories is of a grandmother telling a story to her grandchild about her childhood. "We used to skate outside on a pond," said the grandmother, "and I had a pony named Tobo, and a tire swing that hung from a tree in the backyard. . . ."

"Wow," said the little girl after a while. "I wish I'd gotten to know you sooner!"

Perhaps Jacob's grandsons felt the same way. In Genesis 48, the old patriarch gathered his sons and grandsons around him and he blessed them and told them his past history: "God Almighty appeared to me at Luz in the land of Canaan and blessed me," he said (v. 3). Jacob went on to relate the story of his relationship with God and the spiritual legacy he was passing down to them. It was a recital that was remembered and later committed to writing, and it became the means of passing on the heritage of Abraham's seed to a thousand generations.

You're in a unique position to tell your grandchildren where they come from—and where God has brought your family. Seize every opportunity to give them the gift of knowing their heritage.

Laugh Lines

A teacher asked her class on one occasion what each of them wanted to become when they grew up. One boy said, "President." Another said, "I want to be a fireman." A third said, "I want to be a teacher." One by one they answered until they came to Billy. When they came to Billy's turn, the teacher said, "Billy, what do you want to be when you grow up?" He said, "I want to be possible."

The teacher looked at him with a question mark on her face. She said, "What do you mean you want to be possible? He said, "Well, my mom is always telling me I'm impossible. When I grow up, I want to become possible."

•

PAYBACK TIME!

The boy had just received his brand new driver's license. The family joyously follows him out to the driveway and climbs into the car. He is going to take them for a ride for the first time. Dad immediately heads for the back seat, directly behind the newly minted driver.

"I'll bet you're back there to get a change of scenery after all those months of sitting in the front passenger seat teaching me how to drive," says the beaming boy to his father.

"Nope," comes Dad's reply. "I'm gonna sit here and kick the back of your seat as you drive, just like you've been doing to me all these years."

A Loving Legacy

Use these pages to pass along lessons to your grandchildren.

When I was young, I dreamed about being . . .

_____

_____

_____

_____

Through trials in my life, I learned:

_____

_____

_____

_____

My parents felt strongly about:

_____

_____

_____

_____

Of all my personality traits, I hope my family will remember this about me:

_____

_____

_____

_____

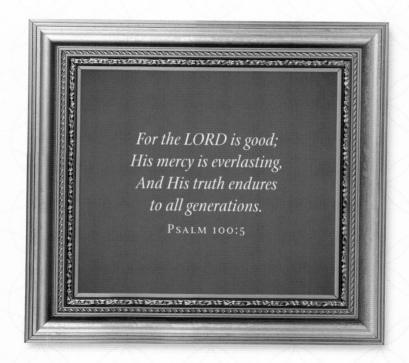

For the LORD is good;
His mercy is everlasting,
And His truth endures
to all generations.

PSALM 100:5

A Prayer from the Heart

Dear Heavenly Father, I know that You show Your faithfulness throughout generations. In my own life, I've seen how You have carried my family and others. You have been steadfast in storms; You have used parents to bless children and children to bless parents. Thank You for the wonder of family. Help me to pass strong values along to my grandchildren, and bless them every day of their lives.

In Jesus' name, Amen.

Lauren Jeremiah, Ryland Jeremiah,
Makenna Jeremiah, and Hayden Jeremiah

Luke Sanchez and Noelle Sanchez

Nanny and Poppy's Brag Page

David Todd Jeremiah,
Alexandra Jeremiah,
Grace Anne Jeremiah,
and Bradley Jeremiah

Special Prayers

A PRAYER OF THANKSGIVING FOR SONS AND DAUGHTERS WHO
LOVE GOD AND ARE RAISING THEIR CHILDREN TO HONOR HIM:

Heavenly Father, I know I didn't do everything perfectly as a parent. I tried my best to seek Your guidance, and You provided grace for every situation. Thank You for loving my children better than I ever could, even as much as I loved them. Thank You that they know You and live rightly before You. And thank You that they endeavor to raise our grandchildren according to those principles. May Your hand of blessing always be upon them, Lord God. In Jesus' name, Amen.

A PRAYER THAT GOD WOULD BLESS MY CHILDREN'S MARRIAGE:

Heavenly Father, thank You for my children and their spouses. I ask from the bottom of my heart today that You would bless their marriages and children. I pray for protection against the forces that might work against them, and I ask that even in tough times they would look to You. Lord, lift their faces toward You each day and continue to work in their hearts. May their marriages be happy and blessed, and may their children prosper. I ask this in the name of Jesus, Amen.

A PRAYER FOR MY GRANDCHILDREN'S PROTECTION:

Heavenly Father, thank You for the gift of grandchildren. I pray, God, that You would fill them with joy, just as they fill me with joy. Surround them with Your angels as they come and go between school and home and activities. Protect them from harm. And guide them with Your presence each day. In Jesus' name, Amen.

A PRAYER THAT MY GRANDCHILDREN WOULD SERVE GOD:

Heavenly Father, I pray more than anything that my grandchildren would know You. Please give my children and me wisdom to know how to share Your truth with them. Turn their hearts toward You. Care for them and let them see Your loving hand on their lives. And I pray that You would fill their hearts with gratitude toward You and enable them to serve You all the days of their lives. In Jesus' name, Amen.

A PRAYER ASKING FOR WISDOM TO BE THE GRANDPARENT THAT GOD WOULD DESIRE ME TO BE, SERVING AS A ROLE MODEL FOR MY FAMILY:

Father, I know I can do nothing apart from You. So today I ask for Your wisdom and strength. Please mold me and shape me after Your own Son's image, and help me be a conduit of Your love in my family. Give me opportunities to make a difference in their lives for You, and fill our home with Your presence when we are all together. In Jesus' name, Amen.

A PRAYER WHEN A CHILD OR GRANDCHILD HAS WALKED AWAY FROM FAITH IN GOD:

Lord, I know that You can do anything and that no one is beyond Your reach. It breaks my heart that my grandchild is not walking with You right now. Lord, I pray that you would remove any obstacle that might be keeping him/her from seeking You—heal any bitterness, remove any distraction. Give him/her opportunities to hear Your Word and develop faith in You. Spur my entire family on to trust in You, especially my grandchild. In Jesus' name I pray, Amen.

A PRAYER WHEN A CHILD HAS DIVORCED AND GRANDCHILDREN LIVE IN A SINGLE-PARENT HOME OR BLENDED FAMILY:

Father, I know that You designed the family, and that family is so central to our development. God, even though my child and grandchildren are not experiencing the ideal right now, I ask that You would work in their lives and redeem their situation. Shower them with Your grace. Fill their home with peace. I pray against bitterness and a spirit of unhealthy anger, and I ask that You would give my children and grandchildren what they need each day to live happy and healthy lives. It's in Jesus' name that I ask these things, Amen.

A PRAYER WHEN MY CHILDREN AND GRANDCHILDREN ARE EXPERIENCING FINANCIAL HARDSHIP:

Heavenly Father, I know that You are the great provider. I know that You have good plans for us. In the midst of difficulty, I pray that my children and grandchildren would seek Your kingdom first. Help them lean on You during tough times and experience Your grace in the midst of difficulty. Keep their hearts free from anxiety and fear and teach them to look to You for all provision. And Lord, I ask in Jesus' name that You would meet their needs and give them comfort. Thank You in advance for Your blessings, Amen.

A PRAYER FOR GRANDPARENTS WHO ARE RAISING THEIR GRANDCHILDREN:

Lord God, I sometimes feel overwhelmed by my responsibilities. I thought I was done raising children, and now circumstances have thrust me back into a parenting role. Lord, I am not up to this task in my own strength. So I pray that You would come and guide me. Give me wisdom to face each day's questions and decisions. Fill me with Your love so that I can share it with my grandchildren. And God, be their perfect Father. Guide us all each day of our lives. In Jesus' name, Amen.

Dr. David Jeremiah
is the senior pastor
of Shadow Mountain
Community Church in
El Cajon, California.
He is the host of the
internationally syndicated
radio and television
program, *Turning
Point,* which is heard
and seen on hundreds
of stations around the

David and Donna Jeremiah with their grandchildren!

world each week. Dr. Jeremiah has authored many books including *Captured by Grace, My Heart's Desire, Hopeful Parenting, Why the Nativity?,* and his most recent best-selling book on prophecy, *What in the World Is Going On?*